CHILDREN'S LITERATURE IN SWEDEN

Boel Westin

The Swedish Institute

Editor's note
A book title given in English in brackets indicates that the work has been published in English translation. Where an English title is given within quotation marks and in brackets, this indicates that the work has not appeared in English.

© 1991, 1996 Boel Westin and the Swedish Institute
Second, revised edition
Original translation by Stephen Croall
Supplementary translation by Hugh Rodwell
Design by Eva Lena Johansson
Cover picture by Gunna Grähs from *Nusse-kudden,* Håkan
Jaensson/Arne Norlin, Alfabeta 1984
Printed in Sweden by Gummessons Tryckeri AB
ISBN 91-520-0384-1

Boel Westin, Ph.D., is an associate professor at the Department of Comparative Literature, University of Stockholm.

CONTENTS

PREFACE

Children's Literature in Sweden was written in response to the request from the Swedish Institute for a short survey of Swedish children's literature. Here it should be noted that the expression "children's literature" includes books for young adults as well as children's novels, poetry and picture books for small children. I also pay special attention to children's book illustration, by tradition a highly-developed field in Sweden.

My task has not been easy, since the 400-year history of Swedish children's literature is still waiting to be more thoroughly investigated. For the latest years, I have tried to present trends and characterize some of the new writers. Ultimately this is what I myself wish to introduce to an international readership.

I would like to thank those who have contributed to the making of this volume. My particular thanks are due to director Sonja Svensson and librarian Lena Törnqvist at the Swedish Institute for Children's Books for their help and constructive comments.

Stockholm, February 1991
Boel Westin

Preface to the second edition.

In the five years since this book was written, much of the more recent writing has struck out in new directions. New writers have made a triumphant entrance, and a younger generation of illustrators has begun to make itself known. Perhaps now more than ever, Swedish children's literature will be able to make its voice heard above the background roar of world literature.

In this second edition of *Children's Literature in Sweden*, the text has been supplemented and revised where this has seemed necessary. Completely new sections have been added to the concluding chapter, which now extends to 1995.

Stockholm, November 1995
Boel Westin

CHILDREN'S LITERATURE IN SWEDEN

Literature for children has long had an educational, fostering aim. Well into the 19th century, children's books sought primarily to impress upon their young readers good morals, proper manners and a sense of religion. In Sweden it was not until the turn of the twentieth century that children's literature began to respond to the needs of children rather than adults.

This may seem surprising in view of the fact that in the international field of children's literature Sweden today enjoys a considerable reputation, with Astrid Lindgren as the leading name. As far back as 1958 she was awarded the prestigious H C Andersen Medal by the International Board on Books for Young People (IBBY). This "Nobel Prize" for children's literature was later awarded to the Finno-Swedish author and artist, Tove Jansson (1966) and to Maria Gripe (1974).

But children's literature in Swedish is not associated solely with these internationally-known authors. During the 1960s and 1970s, books for young adults became a literary export as a result of their frankness and ability to deal with contemporary issues important to young people. Modern Swedish picture books maintain high standards and several illustrators have received awards. Ulf Löfgren won the coveted Grand Prix at the Illustrators' Biennale in Bratislava (BIB) in 1977 and two representatives of the new generation of illustrators of the 1980s, Eva Eriksson and Anna Höglund, have also been honoured. Swedish picture books also won acclaim in the early 1990s, with Pija Lindenbaum and Gunilla Kvarnström receiving Unicef's Illustrators of the Year Award in 1993.

Indeed it is in the picture book that one of the most interesting developments in Swedish children's literature occurred during the 1980s, and above all in the illustrations themselves. The urge to experiment with form and aesthetic refinement is evident, while at the same time a solidly realistic and narrative tradition that began with Elsa Beskow has been continued.

Pippi was given visual shape by the Danish-born illustrator Ingrid Vang Nyman (1916–59), one of Astrid Lindgren's earliest illustrators. From Pippi Långstrump, *Rabén & Sjögren, Stockholm 1945.*

No longer the exclusive preserve of small children, picture books are increasingly aimed at a variety of age groups.

In the transition from the 1980s to the 1990s, books for young adults also underwent change. They became more open to broader social issues and in their narrative patterns and choice of themes they tended to merge in part with adult literature. The narrative picture book for younger children developed into a genre in its own right, with many of these apparently simple books appealing as much to adults as to children.

In general, then, children's books in Sweden nowadays address themselves much less categorically to a specific readership. This has both advantages and disadvantages. Naturally a children's book must first and foremost satisfy the child. At the same time it is difficult to see how innovation can occur unless the frames of reference are extended. In fact, the basic idea of compartmentalizing literature according to the age of its readers is now being called into question.

It is also true to say that in Sweden today, books for children and young people have a very different literary standing than previously. In the 1980s and 1990s, children's literature came to play a greater part in the public discussion of culture in general. Prominent among those laying the foundations for this new role were Lennart Hellsing, who worked as a critic of children's literature for many years, and above all Astrid Lindgren. The latter's many-faceted authorship as well as her more than twenty years as a publishing editor have left their indelible mark on children's literature in Sweden, ever since the pioneering book about *Pippi Långstrump* (Pippi Longstocking) was published in 1945. The arrival of this "child of the century", as Pippi has been so aptly labelled, ushered in the modern age of Swedish children's literature. Up until the turn of the century, children's books in Sweden had largely been an educational concern.

The first Swedish children's books

The 400-year history of Swedish children's books began with an adaptation of the German priest Konrad Portas's homily on maidenhood for young women. *Een sköön och härligh jungfrw speghel* was published in 1591. During the next century, 40-odd books for children came out in Sweden, mostly translations of religious texts, fables and books on courtesy. Among the few original Swedish works of the time were a special children's bible by Haquin Spegel (1684) and a couple of works by Petrus Johannis Rudbeckius (1624) with instructive tales addressed to the youth of Sweden.

A budding interest in the aesthetic side of a child's upbringing can eventually be discerned, however. John Locke's well-known publication, *Some Thoughts Concerning Education* (1693), was translated into Swedish in 1709. But his reflections on the power of the imagination and the importance of stimulating a child's desire to read did not have an immediate impact in Sweden. Publication of children's books remained scant, with less than 250 titles having appeared by the year 1800.

Swedish children's literature moves towards the 20th century

During the Enlightenment there appeared a number of children's books that had more than purely educational ambitions. In accordance with the custom of the times, instruction and amusement were to be combined. Books on morals and manners continued to dominate, but in the mid-1700s a more playful educational approach gained a foothold. Literary output in Sweden consisted mainly of translations from French and German, but one of the few original Swedish works of the day also found a foreign readership. *Utkast af en gammal mans dageliga bref, under dess sjukdom, til en späd prints* (Letters from an Old Man to a Young Prince), 1751, was an abbreviated edition of didactic texts in letter form addressed to the future king Gustav III and written by Carl Gustaf Tessin (1695–1770). One of the innovations of this era was the periodical specifically for children and young people. Sweden was a pioneer in this field, its first children's magazine appearing as early as 1766.

During the first half of the 19th century, folklorists in Sweden, as elsewhere, documented the story-telling tradition that flourished among the common people. *Svenska fornsånger* ("Swedish Songs of Yore"),1834–42, and *Svenska folksagor och äfventyr* ("Swedish Folk and Fairy Tales"), 1844–49, were among the works that led to new genres such as the fairy tale and rhymes finding their way into children's literature. This rich material lives on today in various forms and contexts. The desire

Jenny Nyström's Barnkammarens bok *(1882), a collection of nursery rhymes, was the first original Swedish picture book.*

to maintain a dialogue with tradition and pass on a cultural heritage is an important feature of modern children's literature in Sweden. This trend was particularly noticeable in the 1980s, which brought a string of anthologies mixing older texts with new.

11

During the latter decades of the 19th century, the Finno-Swedish writer, Zacharias Topelius (1818–98), exercised a major influence on Swedish children's literature. His numerous songs, fairy tales and plays collected in *Läsning för barn* ("Reading for Children"), 8 vols, 1865–96, pedagogically combine everyday drama with romantic flights of the imagination. Topelius's texts always place the child at the centre, which was quite new in those days. In 1871 came the publication of what was to be the first children's literary classic in Sweden, *Lille Viggs äfventyr på julafton* ("The Adventures of Little Vigg on Christmas Eve") by Viktor Rydberg (1828–1895), an ambiguous dream narrative about a boy's moral growth. It was later published in an illustrated version (1875) and translated into English, French and German.

Lasse, bunden vid en stol,
gnäller som en spräckt fiol,
håret far i backen,
slät och fin blir nacken.

In Ottilia Adelborg's charming homage to the virtues of cleanliness, Pelle Snygg och barnen i Snaskeby *(Bonniers, Stockholm 1896), clean surfaces and gentle pastel colours harmonize with the message of the tale.*

Elsa Beskow and the new Swedish picture book

The time was now ripe for picture books that were wholly Swedish. Improved printing techniques were one prerequisite, another was the reaction against the characterless, mass-produced illustrations for children imported from Germany and England. People started to borrow from folklore, especially nursery rhymes, and depict children playing in natural settings that were recognizably Swedish. Jenny Nyström (1854–1946) led the way with *Barnkammarens bok* ("The Nursery Book") in 1882 and also illustrated the two-volume *Svenska barnboken* ("The Swedish Children's Book") in 1886–87, with texts collected by the folklorist Johan Nordlander (1853–1934).

Another pioneer of fundamental importance in the development of Swedish picture books was Ottilia Adelborg (1855–1936). Her output was small but highly interesting, especially *Pelle Snygg och barnen i Snaskeby* (Clean Peter and the Children of Grubbylea), 1896, a moral tale with comic undertones that has won international recognition. An important contribution to the emergent Swedish picture book was also made by Nanna Bendixson (1860–1923). Her only book, *Skogstomten* ("The Forest Brownie"), 1886, introduced adventure and the deep Swedish forest to the world of picture books, where they have remained. The picture book *Kattresan* ("The Cat

Ivar Arosenius's verse story Kattresan *(Bonniers, Stockholm 1909), tells how a little girl rides out into the world on her cat and encounters all manner of perils.*

13

Journey"), 1909, by Ivar Arosenius (1878–1909), told with brilliant simplicity, is another milestone. Its naivist illustrations and its understanding of children's craving for adventure have made it something of a prototype for Swedish picture books. This classic of the genre has been constantly reprinted yet has unfortunately never reached an international readership.

Elsa Beskow (1874–1953) is the foremost name in the field of picture books which developed around the turn of the century. In all, she produced some 30 books over 55 years. She made her debut in 1897 with *Sagan om den lilla lilla gumman* (The Tale of the Wee Little Old Woman/The Tale of the Little, Little Old Woman). Her final work came out in 1952. In addition, she passed down children's songs to generations of Swedish children, in collaboration with the composer Alice Tegnér (1864–1943). Beskow, too, was originally inspired by nursery rhymes but soon began creating stories of her own. Her books reveal a strong affection for children and nature. A sensitive use of watercolours, detailed draughtsmanship and calm narrative texts

Dream and reality come together in Elsa Beskow's Puttes äfventyr i blåbärsskogen *(Bonniers, Stockholm 1901). Pelle shrinks to the size of a Lilliputian and plays with the berry children of the forest.*

14

are part of her secret. Influenced by the artistic currents of the day she increasingly moved away from the decorative art nouveau ideals popular at the turn of the century but always retained a personal style that is recognizably her own. The book with which she made her breakthrough, *Puttes äfventyr i blåbärsskogen* (Buddy's Adventures in the Blueberry Patch/Peter in Blueberry Land), 1901, brings the forest to life in a miniature perspective, while in the nature epic *Tomtebobarnen* (Elf Children of the Woods/The Little Elves of Elf Nook), 1910, she tried out new kinds of imagery and the light is more subdued, sometimes dreamlike. In depicting nature, Beskow is always botanically accurate and superbly imaginative.

She has been accused of painting an over idyllic and restricted picture of children's reality, yet this has not put readers off— rather the opposite. Her nostalgic eye for the small-town idyll

The forest became a very important setting in the Swedish picture books of the turn of the century and no one has painted it more naturalistically than Elsa Beskow in Tomtebobarnen *(Bonniers, Stockholm 1910).*

and her exquisite tribute to the discreet charm of the bourgeoisie in her five books about *Tant Grön, Tant Brun och Tant Gredelin* (Aunt Green, Aunt Brown and Aunt Lavender), published between 1918 and 1947 are, if anything, an asset. Even if, in conformity with the times, she did not exactly question adult authority, she always found a place for the creative child in her picture book world, as in *Pelles nya kläder* (Pelle's New Suit), 1912. New editions of Elsa Beskow's books are continually being reprinted and she is widely known abroad, not least because of the way she depicts Swedish nature.

The turn of the century

In Sweden as well as abroad, children's literature had a limited following for a long time. The Reformation's enforcement of the catechism had, it is true, helped to make literacy fairly widespread. Sweden was one of the leading countries in this respect. The urge to read had been stimulated by the introduction of six years' statutory schooling from 1842, the publication of a first reader for the elementary school (1868), the growth of Sunday schools and the emergence of religious movements. But in the late 19th century, literary children's books were still the preserve of the upper and middle classes. Not until the turn of the century, when the literary market began to expand and elementary-school teachers launched various projects to promote reading, did children's literature reach the children of the common people.

This period also represents a turning-point in Swedish children's literature. Several foreign specialists had been emphasizing the importance of taking an aesthetic view of education, and in Sweden the cry was taken up by the influential Ellen Key (1849–1926). In 1900 she issued a famous manifesto significantly entitled *Barnets århundrade* (The Century of the Child). A more artistic and literary approach to children's books now becomes discernible.

John Bauer's picture of Bianca Maria, the princess who has been snatched by the trolls, is one of his illustrations for a fairy tale by Helena Nyblom which appeared in the 1913 volume of Bland tomtar och troll.

The important role played by the country's elementary teachers in this process can not be emphasized enough. School became a vital new channel for literature (the first children's library was not opened until 1911). Low-priced quality literature for children became available on a regular basis through *Barnbiblioteket Saga*, an influential publisher's series that had been launched in 1899 and would continue until 1954. Christmas annuals and magazines now became a forum for a growing body of writers and, to an even greater extent, illustrators. Among them was the legendary John Bauer (1882–1918). In an annual collection of fairy tales, *Bland tomtar och troll* ("Among

Brownies and Trolls"), he created a deeply evocative and richly contrasting imagery that generations of Swedes since 1907 have come to equate with the world of fairy tales. His pictures of the meetings between trolls and humans in Swedish nature live on today whereas the texts they illustrated have practically been forgotten. The many fairy tale writers of the period emphasized virtues such as uprightness and being content with one's lot. The few whose work has survived—Helena Nyblom (1843–1926), Anna Wahlenberg (1858–1933) and Anna Maria Roos (1862–1938)—range over a broader symbolic spectrum.

Furthermore, the teaching profession initiated a major reader project for schools. Sweden's geography, nature and history were to be presented in literary form by the foremost writers of the day. One of these books proved to be an educational and literary masterpiece, *Nils Holgerssons underbara resa genom Sverige* (The Wonderful Adventures of Nils), 1906–07, by Selma Lagerlöf (1858–1940), who later won the Nobel Prize for Literature. Intended as a geography reader for nine-year-olds, in the event it assumed completely different dimensions. This world-famous Swedish children's book, translated into 30-odd languages, is in equal measure the tale of a child's moral development and a many-sided, imaginative account of Sweden and its people.

Among the better-known works of this period is also *Barnen ifrån Frostmofjället* (Children of the Moor), 1907, by Laura Fitinghoff (1848–1908), a naturalistic story about the struggle of seven orphans to survive and stay together. Up to then, poor children had chiefly served to illustrate the charitableness of the upper classes. The text seethes with social pathos, and readers today might find the moral of the story rather overwhelming. Never lacking in popular appeal, the book has appeared in 30-odd editions and been translated into ten languages.

In 1931, Selma Lagerlöf's Nils Holgerssons underbara resa genom Sverige *appeared with the now classic illustrations by Bertil Lybeck (1887–1945).*

Towards a new era—tradition and innovation between 1910 and 1945

The period between the turn of the century and the debuts of Astrid Lindgren, Lennart Hellsing and Tove Jansson in the mid-1940s is often regarded as a time of retrospection. Between these two golden ages Swedish children's literature did indeed consist mainly of collections of fairy tales and conventional stories about upper-class children on their summer holidays, at least to start with. Bourgeois ideals reigned more or less supreme, social realism was conspicuously lacking. Little in the way of ideological or artistic innovation was forthcoming until the 1920s.

But interest in children's books was kept alive. In the 1920s and 1930s an Anglo-Saxon fantasy literature appeared in translation and became important for developments in Sweden. This literature includes such works as J M Barrie's *Peter Pan and Wendy*, Kenneth Grahame's classic *The Wind in the Willows*, Hugo Lofting's *The Story of Doctor Doolittle*, P L Travers's *Mary Poppins* and A A Milne's *Winnie-the-Pooh*. Neither these imaginative flights of fancy nor the advent of Swedish literary modernism was directly reflected in the children's literature of the emergent welfare state, even if there were one or two signs which anticipated the vitality of the 1940s.

Elsa Beskow's fairy tales, which tended to be overshadowed by her picture books, suggest the modern style of story-telling later developed by Astrid Lindgren. Children's poetry, which up to then had largely consisted of songs and nursery rhymes, found new expression in *För barn och barnbarn* ("For Children and Grandchildren"), 1925, a remarkably modernistic collection of poems by Hugo Hamilton (1849–1928). In picture-book illustration, various artistic approaches were tested, but the simple, child-oriented style of drawing that was the product of the educational advances of the 1930s did not make any great impact until the following decade. A solitary voice was that of Gösta Knutsson (1908–1973), who published *Pelle Svanslös på äventyr*

("The Adventures of Peter No-Tail") in 1939, the first of a sequence of books. These humorous, ambiguous stories about a feline world that in many respects is suspiciously like our own, are still popular.

Books for young adults, written either for boys or for girls, were popular at this time. A couple of the best-known books in this category were not written specifically for young people—*Mälarpirater* ("The River Pirates"), 1911, by Sigfrid Siwertz (1882–1970), which describes rebellion against society and the importance for personal development of both a strong will and a sense of responsibility, and *Norrtullsligan* ("The Norrtull Gang"), 1908, a novel by Elin Wägner (1882–1949) about young women in working life.

The many books for boys published at this time celebrate adventure in different forms, often with a more or less moral undertone. Situating them in Sweden, however, was new. A few books for girls offer a social perspective, but the women's right to vote, won in 1921, had scarcely any impact. Several books for girls, however, manifest a radical, feminist view of a young woman's development to maturity, and have women's aspirations for an education and a profession as a central theme. Among the more unconventional writers of the day were Ester Blenda Nordström (1891–1948), with her books from 1919 about the intrepid Ann-Mari who sets up as a farmer, and Jeanna Oterdahl (1879–1965), whose 1933–38 trilogy about a poor girl's struggle for education is a juvenile equivalent of the contemporary proletarian novel in adult literature, itself a genuinely Swedish product. The girl's story genre reached its literary zenith with a Bildungsroman about the orphan *Ullabella*, 1922, by Marika Stiernstedt (1875–1954), which was reissued as recently as the 1980s.

The heyday of the traditional Swedish book for girls was the 1940s, and even though the genre hardly produced any innovations in the field of Swedish literature for children and young adults, it has had great significance for generations of female

Gösta Knutsson's first story about the cat Pelle Svanslös was originally a radio serial. The book was illustrated by Lucie Lundberg (1908–83). From Hur ska det gå för Pelle Svanslös?, *Bonniers, Stockholm 1942.*

readers: books for girls gave young women a place of their own in literature.

The breakthrough of the modern children's book

After the Second World War, new trends in child psychology and a freer educational approach, prompted by such figures as Bertrand Russell and A S Neill, gained widespread acceptance in Sweden. The child's urge to play and seek pleasure was now to be gratified at all its different stages of growth. In children's literature, the world was now to be portrayed through the eyes and voice of the child itself.

When Sweden prospered after the war and the birthrate soared, the demand for children's books grew apace. Publishers made a conscious effort to invest in this field, the literary market expanded significantly and public libraries were built up in earnest. During the immediate post-war period the number of children's titles increased to at least 500 a year. Criticism and public debate was now founded on greater knowledge and there were several publications which focused on children's literature. One of the most important was *Barn och böcker* ("Children and Books"), 1945, by two of the most influential post-war critics in this genre, Greta Bolin and Eva von Zweigbergk.

Thus the prospects for the radical revitalization of Swedish children's books in the mid-1940s were favourable for a number of reasons. Together they created a literary climate that encouraged experiment and artistic innovation in children's literature: in short, literary modernism finally reached the nursery. 1945, the year in which peace was declared, proved a milestone for Swedish children's literature, ushering in several of the writers who are still active today.

A new generation of writers

The supreme figure in this new generation of authors is of

course Astrid Lindgren (b.1907). She could almost be described as a national poet, as her rich and diverse writings strike a deep chord in the Swedish soul. She is as much a narrator in the Nordic fairy tale tradition as an observer of Swedish society in different ages and settings. No one has been more responsible than her for revitalizing Swedish children's literature and in the process arousing the interest of adults as well as children.

Astrid Lindgren made her debut in 1944 with a somewhat conventional girl's story, *Britt-Marie lättar sitt hjärta* ("The Confidences of Britt-Marie"), but her literary breakthrough came with the books about the strong, independent Pippi Longstocking (1945, with two sequels). Audacious and amusing, Astrid Lindgren tilts at the old brand of children's literature with its didactic view of the child as malleable material. And indeed, some of the more conservative educational circles in Sweden found Pippi's liberated lifestyle hard to digest. She is not so much a child as an entertainer who embodies children's many yearnings. Pippi represents an irrepressible life-force, fusing the dream of freedom with the desire to rebel and seize power and turning these adult concepts back upon the adult world. Basically she is questioning society and its values, and the Pippi Longstocking trilogy can very well be read as satire. Pippi is one of Astrid Lindgren's best-loved creations and by Swedish standards her international appeal is exceptional to say the least.

From the outset Astrid Lindgren displayed her versatility in narrative art. In the trilogy about *Mästerdetektiven Blomkvist* (Bill Bergson, Master Detective), 1946–53, she regenerated the children's detective story, while in the short stories in *Nils Karlsson-Pyssling* (Simon Small), 1949, she experimented with a lyrical narrative style that she would later perfect in such masterpieces as *Mio, min Mio* (Mio, my Son), 1954, and *Sunnanäng* ("Summer Meadow"), 1959. The latter, a collection of short stories, uses the technique of the fairy tale to describe the social problems of the poor in Sweden. The three books about the Bullerby children (1947–52), describe the spirit of solidarity that

Ilon Wikland (b. 1930) has become the great illustrator of Astrid Lindgren's books in Sweden. Her first works were the sensitively executed pictures for Mio, min Mio *(Rabén & Sjögren, Stockholm 1954).*

exists among a group of children in an idyllic rural community. Much of the magic in Astrid Lindgren's narration lies in her ability to try out and blend different literary genres and to develop them both psychologically and artistically. The tone of her varied narrative style is often intimate. However complicated they may be in their construction, her books always possess a basic tension or excitement that communicates itself directly to the child.

Astrid Lindgren has focused with particular intensity on the plight of lonely, vulnerable children and how they deal with harsh realities, often with the aid of their imagination. She is at her best when combining realism with fantasy, as in the famous tale of valour *Mio, min Mio* and later in the deeply symbolic *Bröderna Lejonhjärta* (The Brothers Lionheart), 1973, as much an adventure story as an allegory about the struggle between life and death. Astrid Lindgren is no less intense when portraying children's anxiety and grief than when writing about their happiness and joy of living. Now and then her characters come across as perhaps a little too pluckily intrepid.

As a writer of comedy Astrid Lindgren is triumphantly successful in her burlesque stories about Emil, which began in 1963 with *Emil i Lönneberga* (Emil in the Soup Tureen), and drew on her own childhood. Emil's female counterpart in inventiveness and propensity for daring pranks is *Madicken* (Mischievous Meg, also called Mardie), from 1960. The high point of her later writing is *Ronja rövardotter* (Ronia, the Robber's Daughter), 1981, a novel about love and peace. In this book, Ronia and her friend create a new future based on love—a love that embraces human beings as well as animals and nature. Astrid Lindgren's remarkable sense of innovation has given her a special place in Swedish literature. No other Swedish writer has been translated so extensively.

The love between father and daughter is one of the themes in Astrid Lindgren's magnificent novel Ronja rövardotter *(Rabén & Sjögren, Stockholm 1981). Illustrations by Ilon Wikland.*

26

If Astrid Lindgren has revitalized the art of the narrative in prose then Lennart Hellsing (b.1919) has done the same for children's poetry. One of his earliest projects involved the child in a multimedia experience bringing together word and image, music and movement. *Summa summarum*, 1950, illustrated by Poul Ströyer (b.1923), is one example. In Hellsing's world of poetry the reader is a fellow-creator. His verbal linguistics often derive from Swedish nursery rhymes and therefore do not translate easily, yet he has appeared in at least ten other languages. He

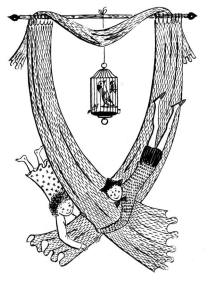

The surrealistic touches of Lennart Hellsing's poem about Krakel Spektakel and Cousin Vitamin are captured by Stig Lindberg's illustration. From Nyfiken i en strut *(Kooperativa förbundets bokförlag, Stockholm 1947).*

oscillates between cheerful nonsense, modernistic experiments in form and a more concentrated poetic imagery. Many of Hellsing's texts have been put to music and become part of the Swedish song tradition.

His first book, *Katten blåser i silverhorn* ("The Cat Blows the Silver Horn"), with remarkable illustrations by Bo Notini (b.1910), appeared in 1945. By his often unexpected choice of artist, Hellsing has enhanced and broadened the art of picture book illustration in Sweden. His frequently surrealistic poetry, which is based on linguistic acrobatics and puns, found a superbly ingenious illustrator in the designer Stig Lindberg (1916–82). He is responsible for the pictures in *Nyfiken i en strut* ("Curious Cornet"), 1947, in which Hellsing introduces the world of his best-known character, Krakel Spektakel. In one particularly unusual book, *Kanaljen i seraljen* ("Rogues in the Seraglio"), 1956, offering philosophical poems of Eastern inspiration, no less than thirteen different artists contribute a variety of pictures, including abstract and non-figurative art.

Hellsing has not only given children's poetry a new linguistic form but also new content, some of which has aroused controversy. Illustrator Poul Ströyer had to put a dress on the nude dancer in the provocatively skittish *Sjörövarbok* (The Pirate Book), 1965, when it was reissued. Hellsing's seemingly disrespectful treatment of death in *Boken om Bagar Bengtsson* ("The Book about Baker Bengtsson"), 1966, also illustrated by Ströyer, was similarly seen as provocative. He is especially fond of the vegetable kingdom, which he has brought to life in several books. A masterpiece in this field is the comparison between human life and that of the banana in the philosphically-inclined *Bananbok* ("The Banana Book"), 1975. It is subtly illustrated by Tommy Östmar (b.1934), who also did the pictures for *Oberon's gästabud* ("Oberon's Banquet"), 1988. Subtitled "A Shakespeariad for Ungrown-Ups", this picture book in blank verse shows Hellsing's constant fascination with tradition as well as his capacity for regenerating his poetry.

Stimulating a feeling for life is one of the prime tasks of children's books, writes Hellsing in a collection of essays in 1963, called *Tankar om barnlitteraturen* ("Reflections on Children's Literature"). Such an ambition marks both his own and Astrid

The famous naked female dancer in Lennart Hellsing's Sjörövarbok *(Rabén & Sjögren, Stockholm 1965) was drawn by Poul Ströyer.*

Lindgren's work, although in different ways. The same may be said of the Finno-Swedish writer Tove Jansson (b.1914). In the momentous year of 1945 she published the first book in the series about the profoundly original Moomin world, with her own illustrations. The world-famous comics began in the early 1950s. Both writer and artist, Tove Jansson bases her work for children on the close interaction of text and illustration. The most visually elegant of her picture books is *Hur gick det sen? Boken om Mymlan, Mumintrollet och Lilla My* (The Book about Moomin, Mymble and Little My), 1952, while *Vem ska trösta knyttet?* (Who Will Comfort Toffle?), 1960, has a more decorative touch.

The first Moomin books are marked by the apocalyptic

29

mood of the post-war era, although in the end it is always life that emerges triumphant. Moominmamma is the central character in the throng of creatures who gradually congregate in Moominvalley. *Trollkarlens hatt* (Finn Family Moomintroll),

The cover of Tove Jansson's Trollvinter *(Schildts, Helsinki 1957) conveys the book's magical, very Nordic mid-winter atmosphere.*

1948, is perhaps the lightest in spirit, yet it too reflects the basic insecurity of life of which the Moomins are always conscious. Life is not peaceful, as the globe-trotting Snufkin so wisely puts it. In literary terms the books differ from one another even if they all play on a basic theme of order and chaos. *Farlig midsommar* (Moominsummer Madness), 1954, is a cheerful comedy of errors but like the darker *Trollvinter* (Moominland Midwinter), 1957, it takes up personal development and questions of identity. Tove Jansson demonstrates her psychological potential in *Pappan och havet* (Moominpappa at Sea), 1965, portraying the various personal crises experienced by a severely decimated Moomin Family. The dreamlike finale in *Sent i november* (Moominvalley in November), 1970, expresses the author's painful leave-taking of the family in the valley so beloved by her readers. Since then she has devoted herself mainly to writing for adults. But it is the Moomin books with their closely observed psychology, their wisdom and humour, that have placed Tove Jansson among the great Swedish-language authors of our time. The books have been translated into some 30 languages.

Swedish children's literature of the 1940s is not just about Astrid Lindgren, Lennart Hellsing and Tove Jansson, even if, in hindsight, they dominated the field to a very great extent. The most interesting phenomena of the period were the tendency towards pluralism and the desire to broaden themes and test new ways of writing. Outside the domains of Hellsing and Lindgren, picture books began to describe city children's daily lives and surroundings, while also continuing to tell traditional stories about animals and nature. The idyllic realism increasingly gave way to a more credible approach to reality, occasionally featuring elements of fantasy and the fairy tale. Among the many debutants in prose at this time were Hans Peterson (b.1922), a writer who focuses on everyday life and who has published more than a hundred books for children. His work varies in quality but his genuine feel for the vulnerability of children has led to a large number of translations over the years. Åke

Holmberg (1907–91) introduced a new type of mystery book with *Ture Sventon, privatdetektiv* (Tam Sventon, Private Detective), 1948. In these slightly absurd detective parodies, form is more important than content and the mystery-solving mostly just serves to heighten the suspense. The pick of the later Sventon books is *Ture Sventon i Stockholm* (Tam Sventon and the Silver-Plate Gang), 1954, not least because of its careful attention to setting. The considerable array of debutants also includes Martha Sandwall-Bergström (b.1913), with a comparatively refreshing proletarian novel about a poor country girl, *Kulla-Gulla*, (Anna All Alone), 1945. Unfortunately the robust tone of this first book is replaced by heart-rending romance in its many sequels.

Harry Kullman provides a worthy finale to this important period in Swedish children's literature with *Den svarta fläcken* ("The Black Patch"), 1949, a contemporary account of city youth and criminality. In contrast to the traditional distinction between boy's and girl's stories, it addressed both sexes. Portraying society from the viewpoint of working-class youth was also something new. But this first Swedish book for young adults in the modern mould gave rise to debate. This is because Kullman sides with his characters and deliberately avoids trotting out the traditional moral pointers. In this respect he is as much a pioneer as Astrid Lindgren and Lennart Hellsing.

The 1950–65 period

Even if, viewed from today's perspective, the 1940s gave rise to an unsurpassed revitalization of children's literature in Sweden, the following decade, more precisely the period between 1950 and 1965, was not as uninspired as it is sometimes held to be. Certainly a whole string of conventional, idyllic stories of everyday life made their appearance, but it was also a time for recapitulating and developing the innovations of the 1940s. Astrid Lindgren, Lennart Hellsing, Tove Jansson, Harry Kullman and other writers continued to produce successful work. The keen interest in children's reading was reflected in radio, the theatre, the cinema (the first Astrid Lindgren film had appeared as early as 1947), new children's magazines and also gramophone records. Several of Hellsing's poems found a new public in this way. Many of the newcomers of the period have become heavyweights in the field of Swedish children's literature. Among these conscientious investigators of the world of children are Britt G Hallqvist, Hans-Eric Hellberg, Maria Gripe, Gunnel Linde, and Inger and Lasse Sandberg. Like the great names of the 1940s, they are all still productive.

Interest in child psychology was rekindled in this period and a strikingly large number of children's books dealt with the creative games of the lonely child. Make-believe friends acquired a firm place in Swedish children's literature. This is scarcely surprising in view of the fact that Astrid Lindgren had already used the motif in her short stories, and *Lillebror och Karlsson på taket* (Eric and Karlsson-on-the-Roof), 1955, was a further variation rich in comic points. Other well-known books employing the same concept are Hans Peterson's *Liselott och Garaffen* (Liselott and the Quiffin), 1962, which has been translated into several languages, and *Fröken Ensam Hemma åker gungstol* ("Miss Alone-at-Home Travels by Rocking-Chair"), 1963, by Gunnel Linde (b.1924), which combines narrative prose with songs and poems. In her more complex work *Den vita stenen* (The White Stone), 1964, one of the finest accounts of friendship between boy and girl in Swedish children's literature, Linde has developed the psychological aspect to involve a symbolically profound play with identity.

Children's book illustrations

In general, children's book illustrations attracted growing attention during the 1950s and 1960s. Inga Borg (b.1925) succeeded Elsa Beskow as an illustrator of nature of the realist school, and

The blue-haired troll Plupp serves as a guide to nature in Inga Borg's books. Animals and countryside are always presented realistically. From Plupp och vargen, *AWE Gebers, Stockholm 1986.*

in several books where she mixes fact with fiction she brings the animal world to life with great insight. Among her best-known works are the series of books about Plupp, a troll who lives in Lapland. The first in the sequence was *Plupp och renarna* ("Plupp and the Reindeer"), 1955, and Plupp has successfully continued his exploration of nature on into the 1980s. Ulf Löfgren (b.1931) is one of several illustrators of Swedish children's books to win international acclaim. Since his debut in 1959 he has developed a highly personal style, decoratively ornamental and sometimes heavily stylized. Like Inga Borg he often writes his own texts. The picture book *Det underbara trädet* (The Wonderful Tree), 1969, a kind of story about the Creation from a child's viewpoint, has been well received abroad. Löfgren has also revitalized the fairy tale picture book. Fibben Hald (b.1933) began by illustrating Conan Doyle and went on to become one of Hellsing's unorthodox picture book artists with a taste for the absurd. With his highly-varied artistic style, Hald holds a position as one of the leading illustrators of modern Swedish children's books since the 1960s.

As with the authors, many illustrators have lengthy careers.

Strong stylization and a feeling for form characterize Ulf Löfgren's drawings. From Det underbara trädet, *AWE Gebers, Stockholm 1969.*

This is very true of Inger (b.1930) and Lasse Sandberg (b.1924), a teacher and cartoonist respectively, who made their debut as a team in 1953 with *Fåret Ullrik får medalj* ("Ullrik the Sheep Gets a Medal"). They have manifestly revitalized the picture book, both in terms of subject matter and artistic expression. Thanks to his naivistic and sometimes simplified style, Lasse Sandberg's pictures appeal to children's own creativity. He also works with collage. Text and picture are cunningly combined and ever since the 1960s the Sandbergs have published an assortment of stories that simply and instructively capture the small child's confrontations with the realities of everyday life. The environment is important and carefully presented. The child is always at the centre, but unlike in many other picture books there are adult roles beside the traditional one of educator. The series about Lilla Anna (Little Anna/Little Kate) from 1964 onwards, *Lilla spöket Laban* (Little Spook), 1965, and the books about Pulvret (Dusty) from 1983 onwards are just a few examples of their extensive oeuvre.

Lasse Sandberg's books about Dusty are among the highpoints of his more recent work. The pictures are often comical, with the accent on action. From Hjälpa till, sa Pulvret, *Rabén & Sjögren, Stockholm 1983.*

A new element in the pictures of this period was a colourful, decorative style of illustration, principally represented by the work of Stig Lindberg, the Hellsing artist. He is one of a long line of illustrators to leave their own special mark on Swedish children's literature, not least on its characters.

Books for young adults

Influenced by the Americanized brand of teenage culture that emerged in Sweden in the 1950s, books for young adults gradually began to find a literary form and broaden their motifs, which up to then had been somewhat limited. J D Salinger's *The Catcher in the Rye* (1951) was translated into Swedish in 1953, but it was not until the late 1960s that its penetrating examination of identity and its slangy prose really began to set a trend.

Ann Mari Falk (1916–88), Inger Brattström (b.1920) and Anna Lisa Wärnlöf (1911–87) all offered contemporary portraits of teenage girls. Wärnlöf's ever-popular books about Pella (1958–60) show an affinity with the Bildungsroman, and as in the case of the other writers mentioned above, the protagonists are middle-class. Yet by today's standards Pella seems rather pallid. A more full-blooded portrait is that of the working-class girl in Martha Sandwall-Bergström's trilogy about the Oskarsson family of twelve children, beginning with *Aldrig en lugn stund hos Oskarssons* ("Never a Dull Moment at the Oskarsson's"), 1952. The characters cook and scrub, bicker and fight, but their optimism sees them through. These somewhat overlooked books are not among the most profound in Swedish children's literature, but on the other hand they are lively, racy and colourful. Olle Mattsson (b.1922) adopts more of a socio-historical perspective in *Briggen Tre Liljor* (The Brig 'Three Lilies'), 1955, a well-crafted, committed account of a life of poverty at the turn of the century. Historical novels aimed at young people were also written by Kai Söderhjelm (b.1918) and Karl-Aage Schwartzkopf (b.1920).

Output in Sweden during this period may appear diverse, but for the most part it trod well-worn paths. Not until the late 1960s, when political debate and a newly-awakened social consciousness radically changed literature for children and young people, chiefly by introducing a socially realistic range of themes, did this field of literature gain any penetration to speak of. But to a certain extent the shift towards social realism occurred at the expense of literary form. The age of experiment was past.

A new reality—the period from 1965 to 1980

The politicized and globally-conscious literary climate that prevailed in Sweden after 1965, the anti-Vietnam War movement and the revolutionary currents that flowed around 1968, the year of student revolt, all contributed to generating a fresh wave of interest in children's books. Their function now was to question reality and furnish information about international and social problems. Representative of this new approach are a number of picture books with titles such as *Här är Nordvietnam*! ("This is North Vietnam!"), *En by i Sydamerika* ("A Village in South America") and *Sprätten satt på toaletten* ("When the Boss went to the Toilet"), all published in 1970. The latter, by Annika Elmqvist (b.1946), is a modern morality tale about environmental destruction. A villainous industrialist pollutes nature twice over, both with the poisonous waste from his factory and the personal waste from his toilet. But, strange to relate, communal spirit triumphs over the ruthless forces of capitalism and a sewage plant is built. The most radical books gave the children a place in the political struggle, whether it involved seizing power at a day nursery or fighting scabs in a little mining community. Children's books were deliberately politicized, which provoked a lot of people.

So-called political children's literature, however, represented only a small part of total production in Sweden, even if it attracted a great deal of attention. Its literary value lay in the fact that it paved the way for books about contemporary problems, in picture books as well as in children's novels and books for young adults.

The political and literary debate led to the appearance of books about social injustice and awakening political consciousness, to reports—more or less literary—on the break-up of the family, sex roles, sexuality and divorce. In books for young adults, a common theme was the revolt of youth against the older generation as a result of social conflict. Examples include *Thomas—en vecka i maj* ("Thomas, One Week in May"), 1967, and *Vart ska du gå? Ut* ("Where Are You Going? Out"), 1969, two highly-charged books by Kerstin Thorvall (b.1925), *Är dom vuxna inte riktigt kloka?* ("Are the Grown-Ups Out of Their

Minds?"), 1970, moulded by the socialist persuasions of the author, Clas Engström (b. 1927), and *Peters baby* ("Peter's Baby"), 1971, a story by Gun Jacobson (b.1930) focusing on sex roles. Maria Gripe's *Glastunneln* ("The Glass Tunnel"), 1969, one of the period's many books about crisis and break-up, follows Salinger in discussing the young protagonist's search for identity.

Death, which by and large has been banished from children's literature since the First World War, now re-emerged, although of course in a very different treatment. The new atheistic approach to mortality is seen in *Lasses farfar är död* ("Lasse's Grandpa is Dead"), 1972, a pedagogic picture book by Anna Carin Eurelius (b.1942) with illustrations by Monika Lind (b.1942). In fact a whole string of taboos that had dogged children's literature were swept away. Finding fresh ways to shock and upset the establishment is undoubtedly harder nowadays precisely because so many norms were breached in the 1940s and 1960s. Be that as it may, the new direction taken by children's books during this period reflects the new social patterns and problems of society. The writers were clearly committed, but despite all the good intentions their political aims at this time seem sometimes too adult-oriented to be really credible.

Contemporary realism in the picture book

A new genre in the field of picture books was the narrative picture story book. With her first books about Totte and his gradual mastery of the world around him, Gunilla Wolde (b.1939) created a new way of telling stories to the very young who have not yet learned to talk. *Totte går ut* (Thomas Goes Out) and *Totte badar* (Thomas Has a Bath), both 1969, as well as later books in the sequence, won acclaim both at home and abroad and have had many successors. Like Wolde's later books about Emma, the Totte books focus on the small child's need for identification and recognition. The figures are simply drawn, the texts brief and informative. Gunilla Bergström (b.1942) is a close disciple of the

In clear line drawings, Gunilla Wolde depicts the world of the young child. The Totte books also appeared in a size which appeals to the young child. From Totte och Malin, *AWE Gebers, Stockholm 1973.*

Gunilla Bergström's Alfie Atkins is one of the few Swedish children's books to have appeared in Arabic. From Vem spökar, Alfons Åberg? *Rabén & Sjögren, Stockholm 1983.*

40

naivistic school pioneered by Lasse Sandberg in her much-loved picture books about Alfons Åberg (Alfie Atkins) and his single father. The first in the long series is *Godnatt Alfons Åberg* ("Goodnight, Alfie Atkins"), which appeared in 1972. Characteristic of picture books in general at this time was a new choice of direction. The emphasis was now on books that took up the problems of everyday life and that also sought to interpret the child's emotional life and its capacity for commitment. The pictures are deliberately kept simple; they are often austere, with colour used sparingly. The books consciously avoid idyllic imagery.

Contemporary prose

In prose for the 8–11-year-olds, too, accounts of everyday life dominate—Swedish children's books are indeed famed for their realism, for better or worse—although approaches can vary. In *Kalle Vrånglebäck*, 1968, Ingrid Sjöstrand (b.1922) describes some typical domestic conflicts. The books about the boy Kalle, his sister Loppan and their sometimes inordinately patient parents quickly claimed a wide readership. Here was a slice of reality that both children and grown-ups could recognize. Siv Widerberg (b.1931), who ever since her debut has been one of the main advocates of solidarity in Swedish children's literature, has often in her writings examined questions touching companionship and common cause. Her lyrical narrative *Klass 6 D Sverige, Världen* ("Class 6D, Sweden, The World"), 1976, is the first of a series of books to examine such issues. Rose Lagercrantz (b.1947) is more psychologically-minded and balances between the real and the imaginary. Her breakthrough came with *Tröst åt Pejter* ("Comforting Peter"), 1974, which, like its sequel, *Räddarinnan* ("The Girl Rescuer"), 1976, portrays in a remarkably sensual fashion the unreserved first love between two rather special children.

The work of Barbro Lindgren (b.1937) is broad in theme and

41

varied in approach, ranging from the cheerful family nonsense stories of *Loranga, Masarin och Dartanjang*, 1969–70, to purely informative books and unadorned poetry. Her autobiographical trilogy, *Jättehemligt* ("Most Secret"), 1971, *Världshemligt* ("Super Secret"), 1972, and *Bladen brinner* ("The Leaves are Burning"),1973, sensitively and frankly depict her own very personal development between the ages of ten and fifteen. The books are in diary form, which creates a special intimacy between writer and reader. They have been reissued time and again and cannot properly be attached to any trend. During the 1980s, Lindgren wrote several picture book texts, but her major literary effort came with the volumes about a boy called Barnhans and his imaginary world: *Vems lilla mössa flyger* ("Whose Little Cap is Flying?"), 1987, and *Korken flyger* ("Cork on the Wing"), 1990. They are in the mould of Winnie-the-Pooh, both as regards their range of characters and the motifs they treat, yet just when the reader thinks he is on familiar ground they surprise him by taking a sudden, more or less tragicomic turn. Barbro Lindgren's penmanship has yet to achieve international recognition.

The new books for young adults

The greatest changes, then, are to be found in books for young adults. Their frank new vein and conscious toppling of taboos made them a literary export commodity during this period. Gunnel Beckman (b.1910) discusses from the viewpoint of the very young woman such hitherto forbidden subjects as sexuality, fear of pregnancy and facing up to a possible abortion in *Tre veckor över tiden* (Mia), 1973, and *Våren då allting hände* (The Loneliness of Mia), 1974. Her breakthrough, *Tillträde till festen* (Admission to the Feast), 1969, which also won international acclaim, skilfully and grippingly combines such typical motifs as the sex-role debate and political commitment with a nineteen-year-old cancer sufferer's fear of death and fierce determination

42

to survive. The book is also an excellent chronicle of contemporary life and may be not only Beckman's greatest literary achievement but also the most powerful book for young adults from this period. In later works such as *Att trösta Fanny* ("Comforting Fanny"), 1981, she has continued to examine different aspects of the generation gap, again from a deliberately female perspective.

Hans-Eric Hellberg (b.1927) is another writer who addresses both children and adults, and he also seeks to break down literary age-barriers. The series about Maria, how she matures from the six-year-old in *Morfars Maria* (Grandpa's Maria), 1969, via the years of teenage turmoil to the amatory 23-year-old in *Maria—kär* ("Maria In Love"), 1982, reflects this laudable ambition. His many other works include a couple of much-discussed books about children's and young people's sexuality, *Kram* ("Hug"), 1973, and *Puss* ("Kiss"), 1975. Another book to arouse controversy when it appeared in 1969 was *Ole kallar mej Lise* (For the Love of Lise), by Max Lundgren (b.1937). It discusses young teenage love in a way that was typical for its time, having more to do with solidarity than unrestrained passion. *Pojken med guldbyxorna* ("The Boy with the Golden Trousers"), 1967, is an amusing look at our attitudes to the developing world. Lundgren has also written several books about the blessings and complications of sporting life, such as *Åshöjdens bollklubb* ("Åshöjden FC"), 1967.

Sven Wernström (b.1925) has produced a number of children's books in different genres. His writing reflects his Marxist persuasion and has an unequivocally socialist thrust, which has provoked mixed reactions—no doubt to the author's satisfaction. *De hemligas ö* ("Island of Secrets"), 1966, is a Robinsonnade describing the origins of various societies and ideologies. *Upproret* ("The Revolt"), 1968, portrays the Cuban Revolution from the viewpoint of the people. But it is as an historical novelist that Wernström has carved out his own niche. His major series about the serfs, *Trälarna*, began in 1973 and

43

amounts to eight volumes, of which the last is *Trälarnas framtid* ("The Future of the Serfs"), 1981. Here Wernström recounts Swedish history as seen through the eyes of the working people, describing the toil and hardships of various characters from the Stone Age to modern times, the unjust conditions under which they lived, and last but not least the emerging class struggle.

Social injustice was also the theme of several works by Stig Ericson (1929–1986). His historical novels for young adults, such as the documentary-like series about Dan Henry, a Swedish teenager who emigrates to America (1969–73), have sadly passed into oblivion. Olle Mattsson's emigrant novels, beginning with *Fem ljus för Talejten* ("Five Candles for Talejten"), 1967, also merit a larger readership.

If Wernström is the socialist preacher of Swedish juvenile literature then Harry Kullman (1919–82) is its socialist debater. His work encompasses contemporary life as well as history, utopian visions as well as sensitively-portrayed realism. He is, not least, one of the great portrayers of Stockholm life among children's writers. Kullman's pioneering book on young criminals, *Den svarta fläcken*, has already been mentioned. *Gårdarnas krig* ("Backyard War"), 1959, penetrates class conflicts in the Stockholm of the 1930s. Violence and the individual, interwoven with political issues, are often central themes in Kullman's writing. Reformism is set against the violence of revolutionary struggle in *De rödas uppror* ("The Reds' Revolt"), 1968, which is also set in the 1930s but which invites parallels with the late 1960s. Kullman is a skilful narrator who knows how to blend excitement and penetrating studies of social conflict, achieving symbolic effect at the same time. In *Fångarna på Fattigmannagatan* ("Prisoners on Poor Street"), 1972, some working-class boys capture a couple of upper-class children, but it is the sons of the proletariat who are the real prisoners. Kullman's final work for young adults, *Stridshästen* (The Battle Horse), 1977, discusses the nascent social awareness of a working-class boy, but the book is above all a superb allegorical description of

44

the mechanics of oppression in a class society.

The writing of Maria Gripe (b.1923) can scarcely be brought under the heading of problem-oriented or openly political prose but her texts do contain streaks of social indignation. Her work extends to realistic and psychologically perceptive accounts of children's lives as well as more fantasy-oriented novels for young adults, often centring on problems of identity. Along with Astrid Lindgren she is one of the innovators of Swedish children's prose. The books about Hugo and Josephine (1961–66), with which she made her breakthrough, address the search of young children for companionship. Two stories of a more fairy tale character are *Glasblåsarns barn* (The Glassblower's Children), 1964, and *I klockornas tid* (In the Time of the Bells), 1965. The five books about Elvis Karlsson (1972–79) are a sharp attack on the family as an institution as well as an almost classic portrait of a solitary child arriving at his own survival strategy and philosophy of life. *Tordyveln flyger i skymningen* ("The Dung-Beetle Flies at Dusk"), 1978, and *Agnes Cecilia—en sällsam historia* (Agnes Cecilia), 1981, fluctuate between the real and the supernatural and demonstrate in various ways the similarities between people of different historical epochs. They also herald Gripe's major project of the 1980s, the sequence of four novels beginning with *Skuggan över stenbänken* ("The Shadow on the Stone Bench"), 1982. These are set around the time of the First World War and in each of them the past keeps intervening to alter the course of events as well as the way people perceive reality. The last in the series, *Skugg-gömman* ("The Mirror of Shadows") was published in 1988.

Gripe writes about lost fathers and vanished mothers, abandoned children and concealed sibling relationships, creating a new form of female Bildungsroman. Her fiction consistently provides a voice for the young woman and her quest for a life-strategy, an unusual phenomenon in the literature for young adults of the 1980s. In the early 1990s, Gripe delved into charged relationships between mothers and daughters in 1930s Sweden,

Maria Gripe's husband Harald (1921–92) illustrated several of her books. His portrait of Elvis Karlsson (from Elvis Karlsson, Bonniers, Stockholm 1972*) has become a classic of Swedish children's book illustration.*

in her trilogy about Lotten and her single mother (from 1991).

The Finno-Swedish writer Irmelin Sandman Lilius (b.1936) is another of the leading representatives of the art of blending realism and fantasy in Swedish-language prose. Most of her books could properly be described as an amalgamation of fairy-tale, myth and fantasy, as in her literary universe reality interacts with supernatural forces. Foremost among her writings is the Sola trilogy, *Gullkrona gränd* (Gold Crown Lane), *Gripanderska gården* (The Gold-Maker's House) and *Gångande grå* (Horses of the Night), 1967–71.

46

Children's poetry

Modern Swedish poetry for children is a small but highly important genre that deserves more attention than it is currently getting. A leading name alongside Lennart Hellsing is Britt G Hallqvist (b.1914), who is prominent both as a nonsense poet and as a chronicler of everyday life. She first appeared in 1950 with a witty account of small-town family life, followed in 1951 by a humorous ABC book with pictures by the Hellsing illustrator Stig Lindberg. Her writings include both prose and poetry, but it is as a poet that she scales the heights. In two collections of poems, *Jag byggde mig ett fågelbo* ("I Built Myself a Bird's Nest"), 1965, and *Folk är så olika* ("People Are So Different"), 1976, she presents concrete, unsentimental, colloquial verse that expresses children's inner thoughts, while in *Nalles poesi* ("Teddy's Poetry"), 1975, she offers philosophically-flavoured reflections on life as seen from the teddy bear's horizon. To this should be added her religious poetry for children, *Jag skall fråga Gud* ("I'll Ask God"), 1968, and her extensive activities as a translator.

Modern and traditional are mixed in the new Swedish anthologies for children. With his teddy bears, Mati Lepp (b. 1947) adapts the traditional rhyme "the bear is sleeping" to the child's world of toys. From Den blå barnkammarboken, *ed. Sara Nyström and Birgitta Westin, Bonniers Juniorförlag, Stockholm 1989.*

The conscious identification with the child that characterizes Hallqvist's poems, often through her use of the first person perspective, is also the hallmark of the new children's poetry introduced in the late 1960s by Ingrid Sjöstrand and Siv Widerberg. But in their case, identification has developed into a provocative protest. Here, too, social consciousness leaves its mark, as in Sjöstrand's *Angår det dej kanske? Fundror* ("What's It to You, Then? Wond'rings") and Widerberg's *En syl i vädret* ("A Word in Edgeways"), both from 1969. The poetry was intended to help the child analyze (preferably adult authority), reflect and take action.

Barbro Lindgren represents an approach that is more lyrically focused and puts less emphasis on social realism. Like Sjöstrand she has published collections of poems for both children and adults. Poetry exposes the dividing line between adult and young readers, a distinction that tends to be made somewhat arbitrarily at times. The high point of Barbro Lindgren's lyrical production is the outwardly unassuming collection, *Gröngölingen är på väg* ("The Greenhorn Is On His Way"), 1974, which uses deceptively simple, raw language to discuss the primary existential questions, often in a meditative way. The Finno-Swede Bo Carpelan (b.1926) should also be mentioned here. He switches from nonsense verse to deeply serious poetry and intense expressiveness, as in the portentous *Måla himlen* ("Paint the Sky"), 1988. In the same year Birgitta Gedin (b.1929) published *Blåtira, kattguld och sidensvans* ("Black-Eye, Cat-Gold and Silk-Tail"), in which the usual, commonplace preoccupations of children's poetry are for once combined with a sensually positive poetic style.

In two volumes of poetry, Eva Wikander (b. 1947) depicts the confrontation between nature and civilization from an animal's point of view. *Djungelsången* ("Song of the Jungle"), 1992, may be characterized as a miniature epic. Anthologies of recent poetry for children were published in the early 1990s, and a number of new writers showed an interest in poetic forms of expression. Poetry for children may also be found in picture book texts, which are frequently lyrical in form. An example of this is *Pojken och Stjärnan* ("The Boy and the Star"), 1991, by Barbro Lindgren, illustrated by Anna-Clara Tidholm.

A new narrative trend— reflections on the years between 1980 and 1995

After problem-oriented realism, political debate and the chronicling of contemporary life, fairy tales and fantasy came back into fashion towards the end of the 1970s. This was partly a reaction to a growing conformity and the routine repetition of contemporary topics. Books for young adults especially had become stuck in a literary cul-de-sac and were subjected to tough criticism. Narrative art, then, returned to the fore and Swedish children's literature in the 1980s was characterized to a high degree by a literary and artistic search for new forms of expression. It also shares with adult literature a freshly-awakened interest in the potentiality of language.

This trend continued into the 1990s, when the narrative became even more central. A poetically flavoured prose was cultivated by many new writers and there was in general a marked desire to experiment with new narrative techniques and genres. An orientation towards a cinematic and visual narrative style characterized a number of pioneering books, some of which were also dramatized and made into films. This applies to books for young adults as well as picture books. In general, children's literature began to manifest a more explicit and conscious interplay between various narrative media than was previously the case. The ongoing dialogue with the literary tradition belongs naturally in this process.

In hindsight, the renaissance of the fairy tale in this process seems fairly logical. Psychology has always played an important part in the development of modern children's literature. The confirmation of the healing power of the fairy tale—how it helps the individual to mature and enter into the adult world—was provided by psychoanalyst Bruno Bettelheim in his book about the meaning and importance of fairy tales, *The Uses of Enchantment* (1975), which came out in Swedish in 1978. In his wake, other foreign interpreters of folk and fairy tales have been introduced in Sweden. But the fairy tale is also rewarding in purely narrative terms. Its blend of realism, imagination and magic provides the writer with an opportunity both to discuss existential matters and raise problems, something that Astrid Lindgren has demonstrated time and again. When the publishing of fairy tales began to flourish once more, both through imports and domestic reprints, socially-critical children's authors also adopted this narrative form. Beneath the magic gloss of enchantment lie commonplace themes that ultimately outline the circumstances and strivings of the human being. However, the authors are often fairly free-and-easy in their relationship with the genre. Ulf Nilsson's collection of fairy tales, *Skeppet Beatrice* ("The Good Ship Beatrice"), 1992, represents a new kind of fairy tale narrative balancing between fantasy and realism. Writers of adult literature, too, displayed interest in the fairy tale genre— one can even talk about a separate group of fairy tale novels for grown-ups.

Equally striking is the interest in fantasy literature shown during this period. Throughout the 1980s, voyages in time and space to alien worlds, where the laws of reality are suspended and the struggle between good and evil can be enacted, retained their grip on the reading public. As in the 1920s and 1930s, this literature consisted mostly of Anglo-American translations, but all too often it was a question of quantity rather than quality. One of the few Swedish authors in this field is Sven Christer Swahn (b.1933), who staked out his own territory with *Havsporten* ("Ocean Gateway"), 1970, and some later books. The occasional Swedish writer of fantasy appeared during the 1980s and 1990s, but the leading names today, and probably for some time to come, remain Astrid Lindgren and Maria Gripe.

Fantasy and the fairy tale have without doubt had an impact on Sweden's current literary output as a whole, yet most of the new writers are to be found at the interface between fantasy and realism. Contemporary life has by no means vanished, but realism seeks new forms of literary expression. So for instance the absurd aspects of human existence are exposed by means of humour and farce and the nature of evil is analyzed within the structure of the psychological thriller. History can be brought to bear on the present, lending new insights, and the prose of this period shows a clear retrospective tendency, which is also apparent in Swedish adult literature. Several women writers of children's literature have devoted themselves to reconstructions of childhood, usually their own, in more or less fictitious form. In the 1990s the trend has come to embrace a number of male writers, too.

The historical novel for young adults has also made a decisive comeback. This development, too, can be attributed to the current wave of retrospection, combining fact with fiction, but is doubtless also the result of a freshly-awakened interest in history after a period in which it was largely ignored.

In the 1980s and 1990s, two fundamental thematic structures in realistic children's and young adults' literature—the quest for identity and the portrayal of friendship—have been presented from a new perspective. A controversial trend in books for young adults emerged: idyllophobia, that is, the tendency to depict darkness, violence, the extreme and the tragic. Harmonious solutions are repudiated. Conflicts, existential questions and the quest for identity are often related to a desire for belonging and friendship. Many new books for young adults take as their theme the painful awakening from the narcissistic self-reflection young people often find themselves wrestling with.

However, there is also scope for a more explicit and uncomplicated narrative of everyday realism with comical features, and the real bestsellers of the period are the books by Anders

Jacobsson (b. 1963) and Sören Olsson (b. 1964) about the boys Sune (for children) and Bert (for young adults).

A new kind of Swedish picture book

The greatest changes of the 1980s unquestionably occurred in the field of the picture book, which has continued to develop as a narrative art form during the 1990s. Its increasing share of the children's literary market is due to a number of factors: growth of interest in the picture as a narrative medium, a new awareness of the interaction between the text and the illustrations in children's books, and above all a new generation of creative artists who have been influenced by such media as films and comics. This phenomenon recalls the emergence of picture book art in the 1880s and at the turn of the century. And indeed the modern Swedish picture book pays its respects to an older tradition while at the same time being more experimental and complex. It is often interdisciplinary, mixing fairy tales, fantasy and reality in books that appeal to all ages.

Intensity and dynamism are the hallmarks of Eva Eriksson's pictures of this wild baby and its long-suffering mother. Text by Barbro Lindgren. From Den vilda bebiresan, *Rabén & Sjögren, Stockholm 1982.*

52

In Ulf Nilsson's books about Little Sister Rabbit and her family, Eva Eriksson has developed a softer style akin to Beatrix Potter and Ernest Shephard. From Lilla syster Kanin, *Bonniers, Stockholm 1983.*

By her ability to extend the writer's text, Eva Eriksson (b.1949) has gained a position as one of Sweden's best-known illustrators. Her often expressive style, which appeals to nostalgic parents as well as rebellious children, is inspired by the extreme artistic language of cartoons. At the same time it pays its dues to the classic style of children's book illustration—there are clear links to Elsa Beskow, Beatrix Potter and Ernest Shephard. Her breakthrough came with Barbro Lindgren's series of stories about the wild baby, a superkid in the Pippi Longstocking mould, capable of transforming everyday life into an adventure, beginning with *Mamman och den vilda bebin* (The Wild Baby), 1980. Eriksson's rapid line and her eye for changing scenery have also resulted in fruitful collaboration with the writer Ulf Nilsson. The animal characters generated by his texts in *Älskade lilla gris* (Runtle the Pig), 1982, and *Lilla syster Kanin* (Little Sister Rabbit), a sequence of four books from 1983 onwards, are among her unforgettable creations.

Cecilia Torudd (b.1942) made her debut in the early 1970s

but did not become firmly established as a picture book artist until the 1980s. Her speciality is the comedy of everyday situations, exemplified in the books she produced with Siv Widerberg: *Den stora system* (The Big Sister), 1984, on sibling jealousy and *Flickan som inte ville gå till dagis* ("The Girl Who Didn't Want to Go to Nursery School"), 1986, about the battle of wills at an obstinate age. Like Eva Eriksson, Cecilia Torudd breaks with the older tradition of portraying children in an idyllic or romantic light. Her figures are captured in a few quick

Cecilia Torudd's sense for the drama in everyday life is clear in this domestic scene from Flickan som inte ville gå till dagis *(Rabén & Sjögren, Stockholm 1986). Text by Siv Widerberg.*

lines and her comic strips, such as *Ensamma mamman* ("Single Mother"), 1988, which unerringly and humorously record scenes from domestic life, have proved a tremendous success among both children and adults.

Anna-Clara Tidholm (b.1946) is another illustrator who has worked with comic strips. She has also shown interest in the folk tale. Her version of *Jätten och ekorren* ("The Giant and the Squirrel"), 1980, has a slightly grotesque touch and sometimes recalls the art of John Bauer. But she has also developed a poetically evocative imagery, as in the beautifully executed *Resan till Ugri-La-Brek* ("The Journey to Ugri-La-Brek"), 1987, about two children's encounter with death. The text of this picture book about the child's power to alter reality is written by her husband, the poet Thomas Tidholm (b.1943). Together they have created a number of sensitive and lyrically narrated picture books. Recent high points are *Förr i tiden i skogen* ("In the Forest Long Ago"), 1993, which brings to life a vanished age from a child's perspective, and the riotous Creation tale, *Kaspers alla dagar* ("Mr Punch's Days"), 1994.

Comedy and the ability to see things from a fresh perspective characterize the often fast-paced artwork of Gunna Grähs (b.1954). She, too, has been influenced by the visual style of cartoons and comics. She has a penetrating eye for farce and caricature and is alert to life's absurdities, as in the social satire *Här kommer tjocka släkten!* ("Here Comes the Whole Family!"), 1989, written by Katarina Mazetti (b.1944). Her highly personal and deliberately non-aesthetic artistic approach has another, somewhat quieter side, demonstrated in the burlesque realism of *Det underbara dagishemmet* ("The Wonderful Nursery School"), 1987, and *Ture går till tandläkaren* ("Ture Goes to the Dentist"), 1989, both written by Gun-Britt Sundström (b.1945), as well as in her keen visual appreciation of the frailties of human nature in *Nusse-kudden* ("The Cuddle Cushion"), 1984 with sequels, written by Håkan Jaensson (b.1947) and Arne Norlin (b.1947).

Anna Höglund (b.1958), like Anna-Clara Tidholm, has work-ed with fairytale pictures in the past but is now more concerned with contemporary Swedish reality, albeit with a dynamic undercurrent of imaginary elements. She is not concerned with "realism" in its usual sense. Boundaries are constantly being overstepped. Her figures look like expressive symbols, everyday

The picture book Resan till Ugri-La-Brek *(Alfabeta, Stockholm 1987) by Anna-Clara and Thomas Tidholm has philosophical undertones.*

settings can become surrealistically dreamlike, perspectives are broken up. Ulf Stark has written the verse text for *Jaguaren* ("The Jaguar"), 1987. This modern fantasy, a kind of traditional dream journey, features the wild world of the asphalt jungle. Affirming the power of imagination, and above all putting it to the child's own use, is a theme on which Höglund provides a variation in her own picture book *Nattresan* ("The Night Journey"), 1990. Her position as one of Sweden's challenging picture book artists was given an even sharper profile by the Creation tale *Först var det mörkt* ("First It Was Dark"), 1991, and the acutely observed emotions in the tale of two bears living together, *Mina och Kåge* ("Mina and Kåge"), 1995.

Pija Lindenbaum (b. 1955) made a notable debut with *Else-Marie och små papporna* ("Else-Marie and Her Seven Little Daddies"), 1990, a humorous tale in symbolic form about a little girl's longing for a father; she has seven little fathers instead of one big one. The father-daughter relationship is also a popular theme in the new wave of picture books. Inger Edelfeldt (b.1956) develops it to produce psychological thrillers. In her expressively narrated *Genom den röda dörren* ("Through the Red Door"), 1992, the focus is on a girl's emotional emancipation from her father. The fairy-tale narrative structure of *Nattbarn* ("Night Child"), 1994, shows how a child can observe its innermost thoughts; the princess is confronted with her own shadow.

Anna Höglund's bold pictures for Jaguaren *(Bonniers, Stockholm 1987), written by Ulf Stark, seize upon the dreamlike character of the story.*

In the 1980s and 1990s, the everyday realism in picture books for small children, which emerged in the 1970s, has developed into a rich and varied genre of its own, providing an artistic mould for shaping everything from toilet training to defiance tantrums. A significant factor behind this may well have been the rapid increase in fertility in the 1980s (the baby boom), but many new books are characterized by the experimental glee of both text and image. There is also an exceptional degree of empathy with the emotional life of children; the narrative focuses on the individual. Some examples of this are provided by Barbro Lindgren and Eva Eriksson, with their books about Max (from 1981); Birgitta Westin (b. 1948) and Matti Lepp (b. 1947) with Viggo (from 1986); Ann Forslind (b. 1948) with Sofi (from 1990); Olof (b. 1943), and Lena (b. 1955) Landström with Nisse (from 1990); and Catarina Kruusval (b.1951) with Ellen (from 1994).

Finally, a few words about illustrated non-fiction, by tradition an educational genre. These books have acquired a new profile through the device of combining fact and fiction and the conscious use of one character as narrator. Inga Borg, mentioned earlier, is an obvious example. Apart from her books about Plupp, she has together with Fibben Hald produced two biographies for children about botanist and scientist Carl von Linné (Linnaeus), *I naturens riken* ("In Nature's Realm"), 1979. Two other obvious names in this context are Christina Björk (b.1938) and the artist Lena Anderson (b.1939). The gardening book *Linnea planterar* (Linnea's Windowbox Garden), 1978, is one example of their neo-pedagogic approach. Their greatest triumph, however, is the book about Claude Monet's garden at Giverny, *Linnea i målarens trädgård* (Linnea in Monet's Garden), 1985, which has also proved an international success. Monet's paintings, photographs and Linnea's "own" photos are blended with Lena Anderson's colour drawings to give an illusion of unity; the reader enters into Monet's world just as Linnea does. Christina Björk, in collaboration with illustrator Inga-Karin Eriksson (b. 1956), continued her work in the semi-

In Else-Marie och småpapporna *(Bonniers Juniorförlag, Stockholm 1990), Pija Lindenbaum describes the father-daughter relationship in humorous tones. The seven small fathers do between them most of what one father usually does.*

fictional genre. *Sagan om Alice i verkligheten* (The Other Alice. The Story of Alice Liddell and Alice in Wonderland/The Story of Alice in Her Oxford Wonderland), 1993, tells the story

59

Lena Anderson's flower pictures draw upon the Elsa Beskow tradition.
Linnea i målarens trädgård *(Rabén & Sjögren, Stockholm 1985), is*
something as unusual as an art book for children. Text by Christina
Björk.

behind Lewis Carroll's much-loved work about Alice.

Among much else, Lena Anderson revitalized the ABC
book, with *ABC, sa lilla t* ("ABC, Said Little T"), 1994, and
Majas alfabet ("Maja's Alphabet"), 1984, in which her sense of
style and closeness to nature recall Elsa Beskow. She is one of the
illustrators carrying on a realistic narrative tradition in Swedish
picture books. The Swedish picture book has a long tradition of
factual books about animals and nature. Leif Eriksson (b. 1942)
and Lars Klinting (b. 1948) are among those who have developed
a child-related but at the same time strictly naturalistic perspective.

On the whole, the future of the Swedish picture book looks

promising, even if there is a tendency for the written texts to be undeservedly overshadowed by all the visual delights. There is much variety and a wide selection, but there is also a risk that the artistic patterns outlined here will repeat themselves.

Contemporary prose

Modern Sweden is an immigrant nation. Every tenth child has parents of foreign extraction and ever since the 1960s children's books have been published which raise such issues as racial discrimination and cultural clashes of various kinds. Contemporary reality dominates and the prose of the 1980s and 1990s has focused especially on those children whose cultural heritage is twofold. In her books about the boy Olle, Annika Holm (b.1937) proceeds from domestic problems but increasingly shifts the emphasis to the outside world. *Olle och arga Amanda* ("Olle and Angry Amanda"), 1986, describes how two children manage to communicate across cultural boundaries, while the sequels, *Amanda, Amanda*, 1989, and *Någon som kallar sig jag älskar dig* ("Someone Called I Love You"), 1993, portray the ambivalent feelings of the immigrant child when her parents decide to return to their country of origin.

Alienation and the problems facing immigrants are also the theme of a number of books by Inger Brattström, who made her debut in the 1950s. She has well-documented experience of the subject, having made a number of journeys to immigrant children's home countries. *Selime—utan skyddsnät* ("Selime—With No Safety Net"), 1989, describes a Pakistani girl's fight to stay in Sweden and can be seen as a discussion of Swedish immigration policy. Political debate and the desire to shake up society, hallmarks of the 1960s and 1970s, live on in such books, but in general greater importance is now attached to the individual perspective.

A number of writers with immigrant backgrounds have documented the stories of their own lives. Ilon Wikland, best known as Astrid Lindgren's illustrator, depicts her dramatic flight from Estonia in the summer of 1944 in the picture book *Den långa, långa resan* ("The Long, Long Journey"), 1995. The text is by Rose Lagercrantz, who tells of her father's journey to Sweden through Nazi-occupied Europe in her own novel, *Flickan som inte ville kyssas* ("The Girl Who Wouldn't Be Kissed"), 1995.

An example of the literary ideological discussion is to be found in a number of books by Monica Zak (b.1939) concerning the brutal devastation of the Central American rain forests. The style is zany, the humour rife but the message is unmistakable. In *Hjälp! Boan är lös!* ("Help, the Boa's Loose!"), 1987, and *Regnskogsjakten* ("The Rain Forest Hunt"), 1988, Zak presents a well-informed and strongly-committed case for saving these vital forest environments. The picture book *Rädda min djungel* ("Save My Jungle"), 1987, is based on reality. The battle of the Mexican boy, Omar, against authorities and officialdom is authentic and has given rise to an environmental movement amongst Swedish schoolchildren.

Viveca Sundvall (b.1944) represents a different aspect of the new comic approach in contemporary prose. One of the high points of her writing career are the fictive diaries about Mimmi between the ages of six and eight, which include *En ettas dagbok* ("Diary of a First-Former"), 1982, and *Vi smyger på Enok* ("Let's Sneak Up On Enok"), 1985. They draw on recollections of Sundvall's own childhood but the setting is contemporary. One of her greatest assets is humour, not least her ability to reconstruct the directness of the spoken language. In her books about Eddie (from 1991), the social perspective has gained depth. The humour is still important, but the crucial thing now is to find a serviceable strategy of life, as in *En barkbåt till Eddie* ("A Bark Boat for Eddie"), 1992.

Ulf Stark (b.1944) made his debut as long ago as the 1960s although he is usually numbered among the new authors of the 1980s. He speaks on behalf of the modern generation, preferably young teenagers. Stark is a contemporary realist yet one who lacks the gloomy outlook of the past decades. On the contrary, his books for young adults are characterised by a strong vitality, a sense of joy for life. Like Sundvall, he responds to the affirmation of laughter, which is not exactly an ever-present feature of Swedish children's literature. At the same time—as is so often the case with genuine comedy—sadness, melancholy and grief are close. Illusion and reality are woven together in the same way as in a traditional comedy of mistaken identities, and the characters often find themselves in new and for them surprising circumstances. Metamorphosis is a central theme for Stark, and in the work with which he made his literary breakthrough, *Dårfinkar och dönickar* ("Crackpots and Nutters"), 1984, a girl plays a boy. *Låt isbjörnarna dansa* ("Let the Polar Bears Dance"), 1986, is a modern version of Pygmalion, and in the sensitive picture book *Kan du vissla Johanna* ("Can You Whistle, Johanna"), 1992, with illustrations by Anna Höglund, an old man suddenly finds himself acting as grandfather to a boy filled with longing for one. In the thriller *Karlavagnen* ("The Big Dipper"), 1989, the perspective turns from humour and farce to horror and evil. Stark's own childhood provides material for the psychological comedies *Min vän Percys magiska gymnastikskor* ("My Friend Percy's Magical Gym Shoes"), 1991, and its sequel *Min vän shejken i Stureby* ("My Friend the Sheik of Stureby"), 1995. Ulf Stark is one of the leading humorous writers of modern literature for children and young adults.

Retrospectives and the present

As mentioned before, there is a striking retrospective tendency in the prose of the past decade or so. It is manifested in autobiographical depictions of childhood, in which the autobiographical has made way for the fictional, but it can also be seen in books of a more documentary kind. It is worth reflecting upon why female writers dominate this literary domain, since in adult literature the situation is quite the opposite. For example, the male writers Jan Myrdal and P C Jersild have both published autobiographical novels about their childhoods.

Margareta Strömstedt (b.1931) is unique in that she has described her childhood both in books for children and adults, from two different perspectives. She herself has pointed out that the book for adults, *Julstädningen och döden* ("Christmas Cleaning and Death"), 1984, is the closer to reality and that in the children's books she deliberately aligns herself more firmly with her protagonist and alter ego, Majken. The series comprises five books, from *Majken, den nittonde december* ("Majken on December 19"), 1982, to *Majken och skyddsängeln* ("Majken and the Guardian Angel"), 1991. Each book spans a single day and these excerpts from everyday life get their special flavour from Majken's capacity for making reality tally with her own highly-individual imaginary world, something she is not always able to do successfully.

In the 1990s, male writers of books for young adults, such as Ulf Stark and Mats Wahl, have published fictionalized depictions of childhood, and the genre is also popular with younger authors. In Catharina Günter-Rådström's (b.1951) childhood trilogy, the first volume of which is *Av sjömansblod* ("Of Sailors' Blood"), 1989, the child's view of the world is combined with adult retrospection. She poeticizes the experiences of the child, and mixes dreams and disappointments, as in the third volume, *Nyckelpigor och citronfjärilar* ("Ladybirds and Brimstone Butterflies"), 1995.

Among the gems in the documentary category are the picture books about three generations of women in different eras and different settings created by Ann-Madeleine Gelotte (b.1940): *Ida Maria från Arfliden* ("Ida Maria from Arfliden"), 1977, *Tyra i 10:an Odengatan* ("Tyra at Number Ten Oden Street"), 1981, and *Vi bodde i Helenelund* ("We Lived in Helenelund"), 1983. Rich in detail, these books bring to life much of the forgotten cultural heritage of Swedish women. Not least, this record is a

64

Ann-Madeleine Gelotte has documented the lives of the women in her family in three picture books. From Ida Maria från Arfliden, *Tidens Förlag, Stockholm 1977.*

superb example of the picture book's ability to embrace different genres at once. Another example of documentary fiction in children's literature is the trilogy of juvenile novels by Ulla Lundqvist (b.1938) about her mother's formative years, starting with *Hilmas tös* ("Hilma's Lass"), 1983.

This brings us to the more specifically historical book for young people which has clearly been of considerably greater interest to Swedish writers over the past decade than previously. No doubt this is due in part to history's function as a rear-view mirror and as a means of explaining contemporary problems, often combined with socio-historical ambitions. Thus in *Smältdegeln* ("The Melting-Pot"), 1986, and *Järnporten* ("The Iron Gateway"), 1987, Mats Larsson (b.1945) offers an interpretation of the history of the Walloons and their impact on 17th-century Sweden, the growth of the Swedish iron-working communities and the beginnings of capitalism.

65

Hans Erik Engqvist (b. 1934) is one of the critics of the Swedish version of the welfare state, the so-called "people's home". His books for young adults are powered by a sense of social indignation. Among his historical novels, *Flykten över gränsen* ("Border Escape"), 1995, deserves mention for its penetrating and committed depiction of a love affair in the shadow of the second world war.

Ulf Nilsson (b.1948) also has a social, left-wing commitment. His writings are broad in scope, covering books for young adults in a variety of genres, collections of short stories and, as mentioned earlier, picture book texts. *Pojkjävlarna* ("Damned Boys"), 1979, focuses on a group of working-class children in 1909, the year of Sweden's Great Strike. *Det märkliga barnet* ("The Remarkable Child"), 1986, shows greater literary maturity, a passionate and concentrated account in fairy tale form, outlining a child's longing for love and his struggle to win it. In *Mästaren och de fyra skrivarna* ("The Master and the Four Scribes"), 1994, the gospels are interpreted from the perspective of a young person seeking answers. In its mixture of fact and fiction, the novel illustrates the tendency of literature for children and young adults in the 1980s and 1990s to transcend boundaries.

Another currently productive and successful exponent of the historical novel which emerged in the 1980s, with its camouflaged discussion of moral and ethical values and ideologies, is Mats Wahl (b.1945). Among his works can be mentioned *Hat* ("Hatred"), 1985, in which he depicts the Swedish Viking era in the narrative manner of an Icelandic saga. *Anna-Carolinas krig* ("Anna-Carolina's War"), 1986, is written in the form of a warrior's diary; the violence is naked and unadorned. This girl soldier's account of the Thirty Years War can ultimately be seen as a condemnation of war and royal power. The intense drama *Husbonden* ("The Master"), 1985, is about wreckers on an isolated, windswept island in the Baltic Sea in the early 19th century. Against this dramatic background the plot centres on the moral dilemma of a young orphan confronted with the violence and evil he encounters among the people he is forced to serve.

Wahl started out as a contemporary realist, and his work in the 1990s has continued to sharpen this profile. The texts penetrate deep into the teenage soul and often fly in the face of the conventions of books for young adults. His trilogy about the mythomaniac Harry Stockman, beginning with *Halva sanningen* ("Half the Truth"), 1984, aroused the ire of critics who questioned its lack of moral values. Wahl, however, seldom resorts to the traditional device of using a pedagogic mentor to give balance to his stories. This process is left to the reader.

Wahl's intentions are often double-edged. He depicts young people on a quest for their origins and the meaning of life, but at the same time uses these inner voyages of reconnaissance as a vehicle for questioning the norms of society. Social classes confront each other in *Vinterviken* ("Winter Bay"), 1993, while in *Lilla Marie* ("Little Marie"), 1995, ideas about sexual determination are rendered problematic. In this road movie, the female revolt is raised to a fever pitch where blood-bespattered violence becomes the final resort. Wahl's prose unites elements borrowed from the rapid cuts of an action film with poetically charged passages and penetrating portrayals of interiors.

A book that is in the retrospective mould of the 1980s but scarcely autobiographical is *Janne, min vän* ("Johnny, My Friend"), 1985, the noted debut of Peter Pohl (b.1940). The setting is Stockholm in the mid-1950s. The author's unerring feel for the language, mood and atmosphere of the times has already acquired a cult following in some circles. Pohl is also innovative in his disregard for traditional narrative techniques. Two planes of time are gradually merged, the 12-year-old narrator-protagonist switches with remarkable daring between different forms of expression. It is obvious that Pohl has worked with film. The androgynous Janne is, like Pippi Longstocking, an alien child, but the difference is that, as the narrator puts it, the latter has been transformed into a real human being by magic. A person

Sven Nordqvist (b.1946), with his picture books about Pettson and his ingenious cat Findus, has become one of the most popular picture book artists since the 1980s. From Pettson får julbesök, *Bokförlaget Opal, Stockholm 1988.*

struggling for survival, one might add. This deeply moving book about adult society's cold-blooded exploitation of children ends in a nightmare, both for Janne, in search of his lost childhood, and for the narrator, Krille, whose ingrained life-system is proving utterly bankrupt. Friendship, loyalty and love are a matter of life and death.

In the novel for young adults *Jag saknar dig! Jag saknar dig!* ("I Miss You! I Miss You!"), 1992, written in collaboration with a teenager, a brighter and more conciliatory view of life may be sensed, but Pohl's emphatically apocalyptic attitude towards life gets the upper hand in his later books. The thematic patterns, the desire of the young protagonist to belong and her painful confrontation with death, recur in a number of new books. Variations on this theme are to be found in Wahl's *Lilla Marie*, in Gunilla Linn Persson's (b. 1956) poetically narrated novel of childhood *Allis med is* ("Allis With Is"), 1993, and in Katarina Mazetti's philosophical novel of adolescence *Det är slut mellan Gud och mig* ("It's Over Between God and Me"), 1995. The themes often centre on friendship between girls, and a new psychological depth is thereby imparted to the traditional theme of identity. Self-reflection is linked with a new feature—the development of a female identity.

In books for young adults from the 1960s and 1970s, attention focused on the struggle for sexual equality, while in the 1980s both male and female traits were presented for inspection by means of androgynous characters. This venerable narrative technique illuminates a young person's exploration of sexuality and identity. Hitherto, the phenomenon has been restricted to female protagonists, and may be found in the works of Gripe, Wahl, Pohl and Stark; the inverse, the boy in girl's clothing, would still seem to be too radical a notion.

It may seem as if the revitalization of young people's literature in Sweden rests mainly in the hands of male authors spearheaded by Ulf Stark, Mats Wahl and Peter Pohl. Young, frequently male heroes wrestle in classical style with existential and ethical issues. Per Nilsson's (b. 1956) contemporary road movie, *Korpens sång* ("Song of the Raven"), 1994, deals with the issue of whether we have any right to take space for ourselves and our lives in an overpopulated world. Women primarily produce picture books or books for the intermediate age group. Inger Edelfeldt is an exception, however, with, for example, *Juliane och jag* ("Juliane and Me"), 1982, a portrayal of friendship. Of more recent writers for young adults, Anita Eklund-Lykull (b. 1942) and Katarina Mazetti are among those employing an emphatic feminine perspective. At present, however, there is no trace of any feminist reorientation.

Contemporary literature for children and young adults often exhibits intricate patterns of narrative complexity, and the conventions surrounding previously taboo-ridden topics have for the most part disappeared, even if one might still hope for a bolder choice of subject. The boundaries between traditional children's books, those for young adults and picture books are gradually fading. A number of books have been made into films, often for television, and many picture books have been dramatized for the theatre. There is a clear orientation towards visual media in contemporary literature.

The system within which children's literature exists in Sweden is strongly directed towards cultural democracy. Reading and literary appreciation among children is stimulated in various ways through collaboration between schools and the public libraries. Literature for the young is also an important subject in today's teacher-training courses. Several publishers have chosen to promote "easy readers". One of the children's magazines started by the teaching profession in the 1890s still appears today, although in a new guise.

Research interest is vigorous. The Swedish Institute for Children's Books (*Svenska Barnboksinstitutet*), has been an enduring source of documentation and information since it opened in 1967. There has been a Chair of Children's Literature at the University of Stockholm since 1983. Several new studies and dissertations have appeared in recent years, and the main thrust of research at present are the aesthetics and narrative forms of literature for children and young adults.

Nowadays, Swedish children's literature is comparatively

well-regarded. At the same time, it should be noted that less than half (some 40%) of the 1,000 or so titles published each year are Swedish in origin. Despite the standing of children's literature, however, sales of books for children and young adults have fallen (by some 4.5%) in the 1990s, and libraries have been hit by cuts in their purchasing budgets. This has led a number of publishers to cut back in turn. Yet Swedish children's literature is still very much an article of cultural export. Astrid Lindgren is of course the heavyweight in this respect—402 editions of her books were produced in foreign languages between 1980 and 1989. These figures far surpass those even of authors like August Strindberg and Selma Lagerlöf. But even Elsa Beskow and Maria Gripe have been translated to an extent that few Swedish writers for adults can match, and many of the new writers of the 1980s and 1990s have already enjoyed international success.

Summing up, it may be said that contemporary Swedish literature for children and young adults both accompanies and challenges its period. It is distinguished by an enthusiasm for testing new forms of narrative, but those books that will stick in the literary memory will be the ones that integrate contemporary phenomena with a deep feeling for the way young people relate to the world.

SELECTED BIBLIOGRAPHY

Algulin, Ingemar, *A History of Swedish Literature,* The Swedish Institute, Stockholm 1989.

Culture for Swedish Children. The Swedish Institute for Children's Books, Stockholm 1981.

Edström, Vivi, *Astrid Lindgren. Vildtoring och lägereld,* Stockholm 1992. (Eng. summary: Astrid Lindgren. Campfire Rebel).

Först och sist Lennart Hellsing, ed. Marianne Eriksson et al, Stockholm 1989. (Eng. summary: To Lennart Hellsing. A Book of Friendship and Festivity).

Klingberg, Göte, *Till gagn och nöje. Svensk barnbok under 400 år,* Stockholm 1991. (Eng. summary: For Instruction and Delight. The Swedish Children's Book 400 Years).

Lundqvist, Ulla, *Tradition och förnyelse. Svensk ungdomsbok från sextiotal till nittiotal,* Stockholm 1994. (Eng. summary: Traditional Patterns and New Ones. Swedish Books for Young Adults from the Sixties to the Nineties).

Om flickor för flickor. Den svenska flickboken, ed.Ying Toijer-Nilsson and Boel Westin, Stockholm 1994. (Eng. summary: Books for Girls about Girls).

Swedish Children's Literature, ed. Birgitta Steene, Swedish Book Review, Supplement 1990.

Westin, Boel, *Familjen i dalen. Tove Janssons muminvärld,* Stockholm 1988. (Eng. summary: The Family in the Valley. The Moomin World of Tove Jansson).

Vår moderna bilderbok, ed. Vivi Edström, Stockholm 1991. (Eng. summary: The Modern Swedish Picture Book).

von Zweigbergk, Eva, *Barnboken i Sverige 1750–1950,* Stockholm 1965 (Eng. summary: Children's Books in Sweden 1750–1950).